18
October

Your birthday book

Your genealogical tree

Great grandfather	Great grandmother	Great grandfather	Great grandmother
born:	*born:*	*born:*	*born:*

Grandmother

born:

Grandfather

born:

Mother

born:

From the day you were born you became a part of your family's history. We have all wondered at one time or another about our 'roots'. What kind of people were my family? What did they do? Where they rich or poor? One way to find out about your ancestors is to trace your genealogy or 'family tree'. Genealogy is a fascinating pursuit and looking into your own, or anyone else's, can be like reading a good detective story. The first Greek writings were on ancestry while in the Bible there is a genealogy of the world's population from Adam and Eve onwards.

Today however, scarcely anyone can trace their family back further than the 11th century. But from the 1500s onwards people became enthralled by the subject.

You

born:

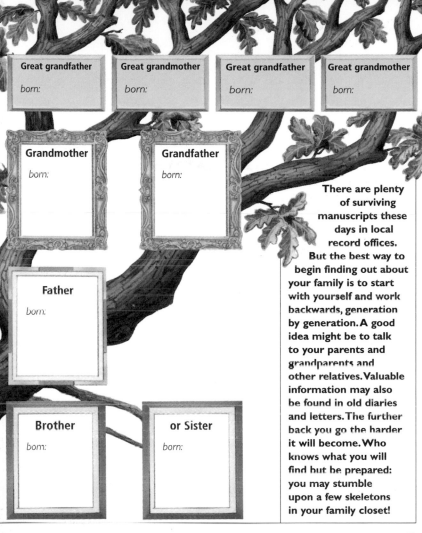

| Great grandfather | Great grandmother | Great grandfather | Great grandmother |
| *born:* | *born:* | *born:* | *born:* |

Grandmother

born:

Grandfather

born:

Father

born:

Brother

born:

or Sister

born:

There are plenty of surviving manuscripts these days in local record offices. But the best way to begin finding out about your family is to start with yourself and work backwards, generation by generation. A good idea might be to talk to your parents and grandparents and other relatives. Valuable information may also be found in old diaries and letters. The further back you go the harder it will become. Who knows what you will find but be prepared: you may stumble upon a few skeletons in your family closet!

The calendars

Needing reliable reference points in time, ancient people began to observe the movements of the Sun, the Moon and the stars in order to establish cycles. Thus shepherds and navigators soon realised that they could use the sky as a clock and a calendar. Thanks to the Sun's regular progress around the Earth, men had a measure for time from very early on: daytime. Then by observing the return of the Sun to the same place on the Earth's horizon, they found another measure: the year, which corresponds with about 12 rotations of the Moon in the sky. The year was therefore divided up into 12 months, enough to lead to the introduction of a calendar which has ruled our lives for more than 4,000 years.

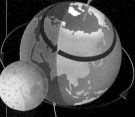

The Sun and the Moon follow different rhythms. Some people base their calendar on the Moon's

cycle and others on the Sun's. Whichever calendar we follow, its function is to give us the feeling that time is passing... and of course, no calendar, no birthday either...

The Earth turns on its axis from east to west and travels around the Sun.

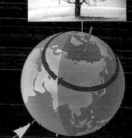

The Earth takes 24 hours to turn on its axis: one day. The Moon, going through its phases (see opp. page) takes 29½ days to travel around the Earth: one lunar month. As for the Earth, it takes 365 days and

The Earth is one of the nine planets which revolve around a star, the Sun, and which together make up our solar system. The Sun is a burning ball of hot gases which is 100 times bigger than the Earth. It is just one star among the hundreds of millions which make up our galaxy, but it is the closest to the Earth.

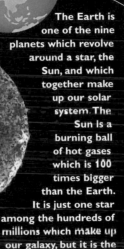

6 hours to travel around the Sun: one year. The solar year is split into 12 months and 11 days. The remaining days are added to the end of certain months: these have 31 days instead of 30.

The two hemispheres have opposite seasons.

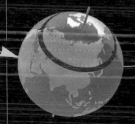

The Zodiac

The constellations of the Zodiac also gave people the means to combine their dreams with their observations and invent magical stories. Very soon astrologers were using the position of the planets in the Zodiac to predict the future. The planets and stars had a significance and secret meaning which influenced our moods, our character and our life. Astrology, the 'science of the stars', was Mankind's first attempt to understand his world.

From their observations of the sky, ancient people noticed that groups of stars, now called constellations, made shapes which they soon named. At first, these shapes helped to identify specific stars, allowing people to navigate the globe long before the invention of the compass. Then they realised that, seen from the Earth, the Sun, the Moon and the other planets traced a large circle in the sky which led them steadily back through the same constellations. As most of these were named after animals, this circle was called the Zodiac, a Greek word meaning 'circle of animals'. The Sun remains for one month in each constellation: where it was on your birthday determines your 'zodiacal sign'.

The Zodiac

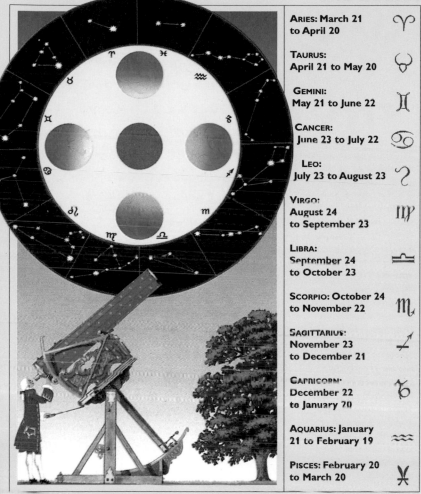

ARIES: March 21 to April 20 ♈

TAURUS: April 21 to May 20 ♉

GEMINI: May 21 to June 22 ♊

CANCER: June 23 to July 22 ♋

LEO: July 23 to August 23 ♌

VIRGO: August 24 to September 23 ♍

LIBRA: September 24 to October 23 ♎

SCORPIO: October 24 to November 22 ♏

SAGITTARIUS: November 23 to December 21 ♐

CAPRICORN: December 22 to January 20 ♑

AQUARIUS: January 21 to February 19 ♒

PISCES: February 20 to March 20 ♓

The planets and their influence

Each of the planets has its own properties, just like the signs of the Zodiac on which they are thought to have a ruling influence. The planet Mars governs Aries, Pluto governs Scorpio; Venus governs Taurus and Libra; Saturn governs Capricorn, Mercury governs Virgo and Gemini; Jupiter governs Sagittarius; Neptune governs Pisces and Uranus governs Aquarius. The Sun, centre of our solar system and worshipped for thousands of years under many names, governs Leo – often called the 'Royal Sign' – and finally the Moon which governs the sign of Cancer.

Astrologers have always believed that the Sun, the Moon and the other planets of our solar sytem have a special relationship with one or more signs of the Zodiac, which adds to the subtle complexity of astrology. Not only do they think we are influenced by our zodiacal sign, but the relative positions of all the planets on the exact day and time of our birth is also thought to influence the kind of person we will grow up to be.

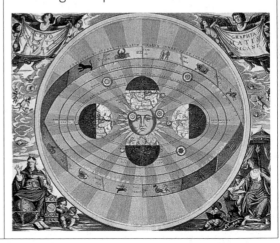

We know that the Moon causes tides in the oceans, and that earthquakes have been attributed to its gravitational force. But from earliest times it was also thought to influence our moods: some people are indeed deeply affected by it – the word 'lunatic' comes from the belief that madness was caused by the phases of the Moon. Many myths grew up around it: in India it was believed that the Moon was the Sun's unfaithful bride, cut in two and only occasionally allowed to shine in her full beauty.

Our solar system, with the nine heavenly spheres.

Your star sign – Libra

The Libra's motto is, not surprisingly, 'I weigh' and, indeed, weighing alternatives can be taken too far by them, which is why they are sometimes hesitant and indecisive. Their ability to see both sides of a question can prevent them from taking firm action and following it through.

Libra is the sign of balance. Its symbol, a pair of scales, evokes justice, measure and harmony in all things. The most sociable of all the signs, Librans are diplomatic, peace-loving and conciliatory by nature.

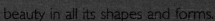

A highly aesthetic and sensuous sign ruled by Venus, Libra loves beauty in all its shapes and forms. Each sign is divided into three 'decans' or periods of ten days. These too have their characteristics. September 24–October 3 is Libra's first decan, October 4–13 is the second and October 14–23 is the third. Common to all three, however is the Libran's need to be in constant contact with other people in order to develop and fulfil his or her private destiny.

But at their best, Librans are kind, devoted, generous, charming and strongly believe that no one ought ever to be alone. They are unusually blessed with special physical grace, refinement and love of beauty. Each zodiacal sign is also associated with colours, plants, animals and so on thought to be beneficial. For Librans the colours are night blue, shocking pink and cherry red; their perfumes are jasmin and gardenia; their gemstone is the clear, blue sapphire; their flower is the violet and related animals are the horse, the dove and the salmon. The Libran's special day is Friday.

The stars of your decan

The third decan of Libra is traditionally associated with the constellation Corona Borealis, the Northern Cross. Those born in this decan can weave a spell over their audience: they are the eloquent charmers. **Chuck Berry** (Oct. 18, 1926), the rock 'n' roll pioneer, and **Franz Liszt** (Oct. 22, 1811, right), the

Hungarian composer and piano virtuoso who invented the 'piano recital', are the music-makers of your decan. **Pierre Larousse** (Oct. 23, 1817, above right), who said he wanted to 'teach everyone about everything', accomplished his aim by publishing a comprehensive dictionary which is of lasting

value. Also filed under research in your decan is **Noah Webster** (Oct. 16, 1758, below), the American lexicographer who with his dictionary

gave American English respectability and vitality. Other men of words include the Roman master of poetry **Virgil** (Oct. 15, AD 70), the German philosopher **Friedrich Nietzsche** (Oct. 15, 1844), the witty and flamboyant Irish writer **Oscar Wilde** (Oct. 16, 1854), author of *The Portrait of Dorian Gray*;

the romantic **Arthur Rimbaud** (Oct. 20, 1854, right), who abandoned writing at the age of 19, and **Italo Calvino** (Oct. 15, 1923), the Italian master of the fable whose whimsical stories have given contemporary literature a playful twist. Other creative people in your decan include **Hokusai** (Oct. 21, 1760), the Japanese master artist whose beautiful waves and views of Mount Fuji are world famous; **Sir Christopher Wren** (Oct. 20, 1632), architect of St Paul's Cathedral; American

couturier **Ralph Lauren** (Oct. 14, 1939), who put chic into casual with his 'Polo' range; science fiction author and film director **Michael Crichton** (Oct. 23, 1942), whose story

Robbins (Oct. 16, 1958). Finally there are two sporting icons: tennis pro **Martina Navratilova** (Oct. 18, 1956), nine times winner of the Wimbledon Women's Singles title, and the

Jurassic Park made him a household name; and Hollywood stars **Rita Hayworth** (Oct. 17, 1918), perhaps best remembered in Charles Vidor's *Gilda* (1946), and **Tim**

Brazilian footballer **Edson Arantes do Nascimento**, otherwise known as Pele (Oct. 23, 1940), who made the No. 10 shirt his own as the greatest football player in the world.

Star of the day

The Italian painter Giovanni Antonio Canale, better known as Il Canaletto, was born today in 1697. His spectacular views of his native Venice made him one of Europe's most influential artists. Many of his early works, depicting everyday life, were admired by the British Consul in Venice, Joseph Banks, who bought some for the English king, George III. To this day, these hang on the walls of Windsor Castle.

Canaletto began his artistic life working with his father as a scene painter. In 1719 he went to Rome to study the works of the Old Masters. There he met Tiepolo and came under the influence of Salvator Rosa. On his return to Venice in 1720 he looked to the city for inspiration.

Il Canaletto

His pictures of the poorer districts such as his *Stonemason's Yard* (1730), though fine paintings, were not what the tourists wanted to see so he began concentrating on the city's great vistas such as the *Basin of San Marco* (1730) and on local customs like *The Doge Visiting the Church of San Rocco* (1735).

Between 1746 and 1755 Canaletto worked much in London and produced some excellent views of the Thames before he returned to this native country. He died in his beloved Venice in 1768, one of the great recorders of Venetian life, and among the first to bring a painterly eye to the new habitat of modern man – the city.

Today in the world

The British Broadcasting Corporation, or **BBC**, was formed today in 1922. Funded by licences costing ten shillings, it was made up of a consortium of wireless manufacturers and, for a small charge, offered receivers for those who couldn't make their own crystal set. By the next year it was providing four hours of programming a day including news,

concerts and instructive talks.

The ownership of the frozen wastes of **Alaska** was officially transferred from Russia to the USA in 1867. In April the Senate had agreed by a single vote to back the Secretary of the Interior, William Seward, who argued that the $7.2 million purchase would reap dividends for America. Many claimed that the 'useless land of perpetual snow', even at two cents an acre, was a ridiculous waste of money but Alaska's rich resources of minerals, fish and furs have since proved that Seward bought a real bargain for his country.

Thomas Alva Edison, the American inventor whose work was fundamental to the development of the telephone, wireless telegraphy, the electric lamp, the motion-picture projector, and the phonograph, died in 1931. Born in 1847, he was one of the few people who truly could claim to have changed the way we live, and when he died on Sunday the 18th at 3.24 am it was the telephone, the telegraph and the radio which flashed the news of his death all around the globe.

Sixty lorries carrying essential supplies for the Allied war effort arrived at Kunming in China in 1940 – the first in three months to pass along the **Burma road** (left). None of the expected air attacks took place and the next day another 2,000 lorries set off.

Scientists James Watson (right), Francis Crick (below) and Maurice Wilkins received the **Nobel Prize** today in 1962 for their discovery of DNA.

Finally, today in 1961, Henri Matisse's *Le Bateau* (*The Boat*) went on display at New York's Museum of Modern Art. No one noticed that it was hung upside down until a month or so later.

Event of the day

In an encounter that marked yet another step on the relentless downward progress of his fortunes, the French Emperor Napoleon Bonaparte was defeated at the Battle of Leipzig, known in Germany as the Battle of the Nations, today in 1813.

In 1812 Napoleon had set out to take Moscow and secure Russia for the French Empire. Despite a series of victories he was forced to abandon his plans and march his exhausted troops back across the frozen wastes. Thousands of soldiers were lost. For the first time, Napoleon's enemies realised that he could be beaten. Napoleon set about building a new army and won notable victories at Lützen in May and Dresden in August.

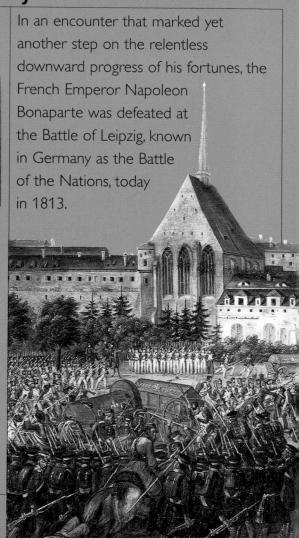

Battle of Leipzig

But he had over-stretched himself and antagonised Europe. In October his 130,000 troops met a combined army of 320,000 Austrians, Russians, Prussians and Swedes at Leipzig. On the third day the great general was forced to retreat. By the time his troops crossed the River Pleisse, only 70,000 soldiers remained. In January 1814 Napoleon lost Italy and, for the first time, his troops were forced to fight on French soil. On March 31 the Allied forces marched through Paris. France had fallen.

Six days later Napoleon abdicated, his Empire effectively finished.

Inventions of the month

Every month, if not every year, sees its own share of inventions, great or otherwise, which shape our everyday lives. October is no exception.

A new style of calendar, known as the **Gregorian Calendar**, after its creator, Pope Gregory XIV, came into existence on October 4, 1582. It replaced the old Julian calendar, created in 44 BC by the Roman general Julius Caesar. The Julian calendar, with its year of 365.25 days was too long by some 11 minutes 14 seconds. This error became measurable in days over the centuries so in 1582 Pope Gregory ruled that October 5 should be called October 15. This change took place immediately in Italy, France, Spain and Portugal, but the new-style calendar was not used in England and its colonies until 1752.

On certainly more entertaining note October 21, 1848 saw an invention of a very different sort: the **can-can**, a dance that delighted audiences at the Paris dance halls where – with much high-kicking and swirling of petticoats – it was performed. No one knows where the name comes from, although one meaning of the word in French is 'quacking like a duck'.

On October 21, 1879 Thomas Edison wrote in his journal, 'Today the sight we had so long desired to see

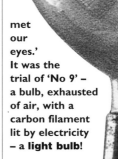

met our eyes.' It was the trial of 'No 9' – a bulb, exhausted of air, with a carbon filament lit by electricity – a **light bulb**!

'What a beautiful thing to have invented', said one of his excited technicians as they sat up all night staring at the light. It burnt for over 13 hours before the glass broke. 'If it can burn that number of hours,' said Edison, 'I know I can make it burn hundred.'

Tobacco heir Griswold Lorillard shocked fellow guests at that year's ultra-fashionable ball at the country club at Tuxedo Park, New York, when on October 10, 1886 he turned up in a brand new fashion style: a dress coat, but without the usual 'tails'. The short jacket, which was promptly named **tuxedo** in honour of its first appearance, went on to oust the old tails and to become what Britain calls a 'dinner jacket'.

The world's first **matches** were patented by Alonzo Phillips of Massachusetts on October 24, 1836. Unlike

today's safety matches, these were much cruder affairs. A piece of wood soaked in sulphur was dragged against sand-paper, thus producing a flame. Book matches, used around the world for advertising and information, were invented in 1892.

Finally, the first **spring mattress** was patented by Samuel Pratt on October 18, 1826.

The seasons

Autumn, for the English poet John Keats the 'Season of mists and mellow fruitfulness', is also a period of change. Life in the Northern Hemisphere starts to move slowly: migratory birds gather in the trees and line up on telegraph poles before setting out on their long journey to warmer climates, while plants and animals begin to adapt themselves in preparation for the coming winter.

The migration of the crane, flying by day and night, is a spectacular sight. Flying in large groups, usually in a V- or W-shaped formation, they advance slowly and gracefully, filling the air with their mournful and disturbing cries. They can cover huge distances, stopping only to feed in favourite resting places. To the Japanese the crane is a symbol of wisdom. During its winter

Autumn

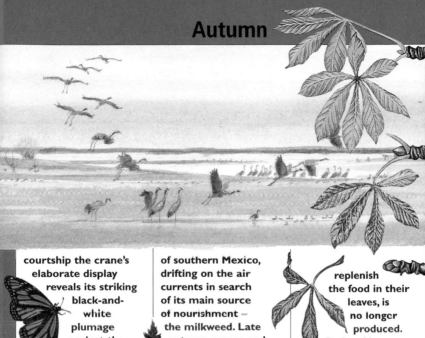

courtship the crane's elaborate display reveals its striking black-and-white plumage against the snow, and has inspired many Japanese artists. The monarch butterfly is another marathon migrator. Before winter sets in it travels over 3,000 miles from Canada in the north to the sunnier climes of southern Mexico, drifting on the air currents in search of its main source of nourishment – the milkweed. Late autumn comes and the days draw in and as the light fades leaves fall to the ground, giving the trees a better chance of surviving the cold weather. Chlorophyll, the green pigment which allows plants to replenish the food in their leaves, is no longer produced. Red and brown pigments now appear and give the trees their rich autumnal hues. The sap can no longer reach the leaves and they die so that the tree may live. Fir trees do not lose their needles as these are smaller and can resist both the cold and lack of light. This is why they are 'ever green'.

Festivals of the month

'Roll out the barrel!' is the cry of beer-loving punters everywhere as they head for Munich's 16-day **Oktoberfest** (Oct. 21, right). The feast begins with parades of decorated beer wagons and people dressed in folk costumes, right down to the much-mentioned lederhosen. The Lord Mayor of the city has the privilege of opening the first barrel, whereupon the serious boozing commences. By contrast, Phuket in Thailand observes a nine-day **Vegetarian Festival** (late Sep. or Oct.), during which devout Taoists abstain from meat. This is accompanied by mind-boggling feats of mortification – walking on hot coals, skewering of cheeks and tongues, and hanging from hooks dug into the skin. **Hallowe'en** (Oct. 31), with its ghouls and trick-or-treating youngsters, seems tame by comparison.

Eskimos celebrate the Festival of the **Bearded Seal** in October; a time for hunters to revere the souls of the hunted. A harpoon, in which the seal's soul is thought to reside, is stood by a lamp during the first night. No work is permitted for three days, after which the bladders of all the bearded seals caught in the past year are sunk through a hole in the ice. Jews embark on a seven-day harvest festival originally called the **Feast of the Ingathering** (above left). Meals are eaten in a trellis-roofed hut called the 'sukkot', which is now also the name of the festival. For Buddhists October is a time of great joy as the Buddha returns from heaven in the **Festival of Light**, his way lit by fire-balloons,

lanterns and candles. Hindus in India honour the fierce goddess Durga, the vanquisher of demons: **Durga Puja** (Sep.–Oct.) involves nine days of prayer and nine nights of dancing when all dress up. In Morocco there are **Fantasias** (Oct. 7, left) celebrating the mighty Arab horses which take part in a spectacular charges through the cities. The most spectacular fantasia is to be seen in the city of Meknes. Finally in Australia, the town of Bowral greets the spring with a **Tulip**

Festival, with over 60,000 blooms spreading a blaze of colour through parks and gardens.

27

King Henry V of England, in his bid to capture the French throne, led the English into battle at Agincourt in northern France on the morning of October 25, 1415. Henry's army numbered only 12,000 and faced a French force nearly four times that. Yet at the end of the day the French had lost 5,000 men with a further 1,000 taken prisoner while the rest had fled. The victorious English army had lost a mere 1,000.

The Battle of Agincourt

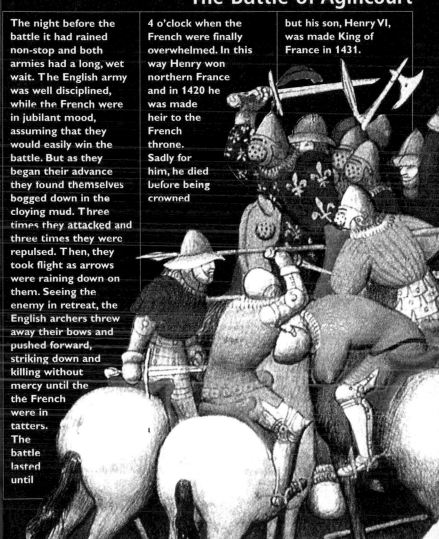

The night before the battle it had rained non-stop and both armies had a long, wet wait. The English army was well disciplined, while the French were in jubilant mood, assuming that they would easily win the battle. But as they began their advance they found themselves bogged down in the cloying mud. Three times they attacked and three times they were repulsed. Then, they took flight as arrows were raining down on them. Seeing the enemy in retreat, the English archers threw away their bows and pushed forward, striking down and killing without mercy until the the French were in tatters. The battle lasted until 4 o'clock when the French were finally overwhelmed. In this way Henry won northern France and in 1420 he was made heir to the French throne. Sadly for him, he died before being crowned but his son, Henry VI, was made King of France in 1431.

'I think, therefore I am,' wrote the French philosopher René Descartes. Here are some of the thoughts people have had today.

1865

That's Article 98; no go on to the next. (last words)
Lord Palmerston (1784-1865) *British Prime Minister*

1870

Old James Jones was breaking stones. He told me how he had once cured his deafness for a time by pouring hot eel oil into his ear and again by sticking into his ear an elder twig, and wearing it there day and night. The effect of the eel oil at first was, he said, to make his head and brains feel full of crawling creatures.
Francis Kilvert (1840-79) *English country parson*

1874

the Jungfrau – This glorious creature is your one object of interest from morning to night...She has such moods, such unutterable smiles, such inscrutable sulks, such growls of rage suppressed, such thunder of avalanches, such crowns of stars.
Rev. T.E. Brown (fl. 1870) *American parson and mountaineer*

1931

It is very beautiful over there! (last words)
Thomas Alva Edison (1847-1931) *American inventor*